Iowa

by Sandra J. Christian, M.Ed.

Consultant:
Lynn E. Nielsen, Ph.D.
Professor of Education
Department of Curriculum and Instruction
University of Northern Iowa
Cedar Falls, Iowa

Capstone
press
Mankato, Minnesota

Capstone Press
151 Good Counsel Drive • P.O. Box 669 • Mankato, Minnesota 56002
http://www.capstone-press.com

Copyright © 2003 by Capstone Press. All rights reserved.
No part of this publication may be reproduced in whole or in part, or stored in a retrieval system, or transmitted in any form or by any means, electronic, mechanical, photocopying, recording, or otherwise, without written permission of the publisher. For information regarding permission, write to Capstone Press, 151 Good Counsel Drive, P.O. Box 669, Dept. R, Mankato, Minnesota 56002.
Printed in the United States of America

Library of Congress Cataloging-in-Publication Data
Christian, Sandra J.
    Iowa/by Sandra J. Christian.
    v. cm.—(Land of liberty)
    Includes bibliographical references and index.
    Contents: About Iowa—Land and climate—History of Iowa—Government and politics—Economy and resources—People and culture
    ISBN 0-7368-1583-X (hardcover)
    1. Iowa—Juvenile literature. [1. Iowa.] I. Title. II. Series.
F621.3 .C48 2003
977.7—dc21   2002012012

Summary: An introduction to the geography, history, government, politics, economy, resources, people, and culture of Iowa, including maps, charts, and a recipe.

Editorial Credits
Rebecca Glaser and Rachel A. Koestler-Grack, editors; Jenny Schonborn, series and book designer; Deirdre Barton and Wanda Winch, photo researchers; Eric Kudalis, product planning editor

Photo Credits
Cover images: Cornfield and farm near Elkader, Iowa, Dietrich Photography/Dick Dietrich; covered bridge, Index Stock Imagery/Leon Pantenburg

The Art Institute of Chicago/Friends of American Art Collection/Grant Wood, 48; Capstone Press/Gary Sundermeyer, 54; Corbis, 38; Corbis/Bettmann, 26; Corbis/Richard Hamilton Smith, 40; Corbis Sygma/Steve Liss, 37; Corbis Sygma/Jim Shaffer, 28–29; Corbis/Frank Lane Picture Agency/Maurice Nimmo, 12; Corbis/Tom Bean, 63; Daniel Hodges, 23; Hulton/Archive by Getty Images, 24, 58; Index Stock Imagery/Ewing Galloway, 35; Iowa Tourism Office, 13, 50–51; Michael and Christine O'Riley, 4; National Mississippi River Museum and Aquarium, 19; National Park Service/Effigy Mounds National Monument, 16; North Wind Picture Archives, 34; One Mile Up, Inc., 55 (both); PhotoDisc, Inc./Photolink/Scenics of America, 1; Robert McCaw, 56, 57; State Historical Society of Iowa/Daniel Hodges, 22; Steve Mulligan, 8, 14–15; Steve Pope Photography, 53; Stock Montage, Inc., 20; Unicorn Stock Photos/Andre Jenny, 30; Unicorn Stock Photos/Greg Clark, 42–43; Unicorn Stock Photos/Nancy Ferguson, 44; U. S. Postal Service, 59

Artistic Effects
Brand X Pictures; Digital Stock; Earthstar Stock, Inc.; PhotoDisc, Inc.

1 2 3 4 5 6 08 07 06 05 04 03

Table of Contents

Chapter 1 About Iowa 5

Chapter 2 Land and Climate 9

Chapter 3 History of Iowa 17

Chapter 4 Government and Politics 31

Chapter 5 Economy and Resources 39

Chapter 6 People and Culture 45

Maps
Iowa Cities 7
Iowa's Land Features 11

Features
Recipe: Oven Caramel Corn 54
Iowa's Flag and Seal 55
Almanac 56
Timeline 58
Words to Know 60
To Learn More 61
Internet Sites 61
Places to Write and Visit 62
Index 64

Hot-air balloon pilots come from around the United States to fly at the National Balloon Classic in Iowa each summer.

Chapter 1

About Iowa

Once every summer, more than 100 colorful hot-air balloons fill the sky over Indianola, Iowa. The balloon pilots come for the National Balloon Classic, which takes place in late July or early August. Begun in 1970, it was the first national U.S. championship for hot-air ballooning. People travel from all over the United States to watch and fly in the race.

People call the National Balloon Classic the Midwest's most colorful event. Each balloon is bright and decorative. Some pilots make their balloons into fun characters, such as the Flying Purple Eater, a funny-looking monster. Some companies sponsor balloons, including T-Rex, the Sinclair Dinosaur.

Did you know...?
The Iowa Hawkeyes football team has a long-standing rivalry with the University of Minnesota. In 1935, the governors of the two states bet on the football game between the two teams. Iowa lost, and the governor gave Minnesota's governor a pig named Floyd of Rosedale. He gave the pig to the University of Minnesota and had a sculptor create a statue of Floyd. Every year, the winning team gets to keep the pig statue until the next year's game.

The Hawkeye State

Iowa's nickname is the "Hawkeye State." This nickname honors American Indian Chief Black Hawk. This Sauk Indian leader lived in Iowa during the early 1800s. He led the Mesquakie, also known as Fox, and Sauk Indians in the Black Hawk War of 1832. Europeans called these tribes the Sac and Fox.

The Hawkeye State lies in the heart of the midwestern United States. Wisconsin and Illinois lie to Iowa's east, across the Mississippi River. Minnesota borders Iowa to the north. In the west, the Missouri River separates Iowa from Nebraska. In the northwestern part of the state, the Big Sioux River separates Iowa from South Dakota. Missouri lies to the south. Iowa is the 26th largest state, covering 56,276 square miles (145,755 square kilometers). Iowa's population of nearly 3 million people ranks 30th in the nation.

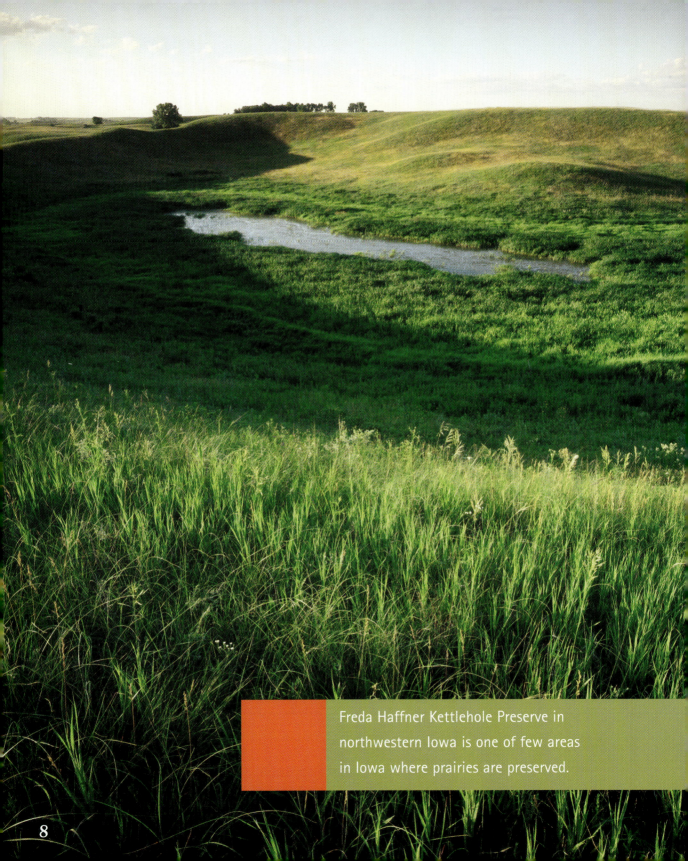
Freda Haffner Kettlehole Preserve in northwestern Iowa is one of few areas in Iowa where prairies are preserved.

Chapter 2

Land and Climate

The plains and rolling hills of Iowa contain some of the world's richest soil. More than 90 percent of Iowa's land is farmed. Some people call Iowa the "Land Where the Tall Corn Grows."

Iowa is part of the Central Lowlands. This large, fertile area lies between the Appalachian Mountains in the east and the Great Plains in the west. Much of the flat Central Lowlands is used as farmland.

Iowa's land can be divided into three regions. These regions are the Dissected Till Plains, the Young Drift Plains, and the Driftless Area.

"I prefer to think of Iowa as I saw it through the eyes of a 10-year-old boy. Those were eyes filled with the wonders of Iowa's streams and woods, of the mystery of growing crops."
—Herbert Hoover, 31st president of the United States, born in West Branch

Land Regions

The Dissected Till Plains lie mostly in southern Iowa. This area of rolling hills reaches up to the state's northwest corner. More than 500,000 years ago, glaciers left deposits of fine, fertile soil called till here. Rivers and streams cut into the plains, or dissected them. Low, rolling hills and bluffs now separate some of the flat land in the Dissected Till Plains.

The Young Drift Plains cover central and northern Iowa. More than 500,000 years ago, glaciers moved across this area. The glaciers leveled the soil and left a mixture of soil and rock. These deposits are called drift. The drift created rich topsoil, giving this area excellent farmland. Most of Iowa's natural lakes, carved long ago by glaciers, lie in this region.

The Driftless Area runs along the Mississippi River on the northeast border of Iowa. Only one glacier moved through this region. Forests of tall pine trees grow on the hills and cliffs of the Driftless Area. Iowans enjoy hiking

Iowa's Land Features

and camping in this area they call the "Switzerland of America." The landscape there is similar to Switzerland's landscape.

Geode

Geode is found throughout Iowa. This round rock has a hard outer shell. When a geode is broken, a sparkling inner lining of mineral crystals can be seen. Geode is rare in the rest of the country. But a large amount of geode rock can be found in the Dissected Till Plains of southwestern Iowa.

Rivers and Lakes

More than 70,000 miles (112,650 kilometers) of streams and rivers cross Iowa's land. The Mississippi and Missouri Rivers form most of the eastern and western borders of the state. The Big Sioux forms part of the western border. Iowa's rivers are used as shipping routes.

Iowa's largest lakes were formed by people. The Red Rock Dam in south central Iowa forms Red Rock Lake. The Red Rock Dam was completed in 1969 to control flooding of the Des Moines River. A dam on the Chariton River forms Rathbun Reservoir.

Most of Iowa's natural lakes are found in the Young Drift Plains. Storm, Clear, and Spirit Lakes are in northern Iowa. Many people enjoy vacationing at Okoboji Lakes.

Climate

The climate of Iowa can vary greatly. Iowa's average winter temperature is 19 degrees Fahrenheit (minus 7 degrees Celsius). The average summer temperature is 72 degrees Fahrenheit (22 degrees Celsius). The highest recorded temperature in Iowa's history was on July 20, 1934. That day, the temperature climbed to 118 degrees Fahrenheit (48 degrees Celsius).

On average, Iowa receives about 32 inches (81 centimeters) of rain and snow each year. Droughts sometimes hit the state. During these periods without rain, crops can wither and die.

The Okoboji Lakes are a popular vacation spot. Amusement parks, golf courses, and resort campgrounds circle the lake.

"Nature was in a most pleasant mood when our land was fashioned. She bounded us by two mighty rivers, here ever to be harnessed for power unlimited."
—Governor William L. Harding, in his inaugural address in 1919

Iowa's location in the central United States puts the state in the path of severe storms. Iowa is part of Tornado Alley. Tornadoes and strong windstorms often strike this area, which stretches from Texas to North Dakota. Severe thunderstorms are common during spring and summer months. Iowa winters can bring blizzards when high winds accompany snowy weather.

A Changed Landscape

Iowa has changed since it was first settled in the 1800s. Native prairie grasses once grew up to 6 feet (1.8 meters) tall. The waters were clear and clean. Farms, cities, factories, and roads now cover much of Iowa. Little native prairie still exists. Loss of native habitat is the greatest danger for animals and plants.

Much of Iowa's fertile topsoil has eroded since farmers began growing crops in the state. Water and wind erosion can easily affect soil loosened for planting. Chemicals used in farming seep into the water and the land. Iowans face the challenge of balancing farming with protecting the environment.

Wildflowers grow in the Kalsow State Prairie Preserve in northwestern Iowa. Most of Iowa's native prairies are now farmland.

The "marching bears" are a group of mounds at Effigy Mounds National Monument near Harpers Ferry. The mounds were outlined so they could be seen from the air.

Chapter 3

History of Iowa

Prehistoric people called Mound Builders lived in eastern Iowa from about 500 B.C. to A.D. 1300. The Mound Builders buried their dead in large mounds shaped like animals. These mounds can still be seen today.

American Indians

In the 1600s, about 20 different groups of American Indians lived in and around present-day Iowa. These groups included Ioway, Sauk, and Mesquakie Indians. The state is named after the Ioway Indians. Ioway Indians lived in villages in central Iowa. Ioway women farmed large gardens of corn, beans, and squash. Ioway men hunted deer and buffalo.

First Europeans

Early explorers in Iowa came from France. In 1673, French explorer Louis Jolliet and French priest Father Jacques Marquette canoed down the Mississippi River. They traveled to what is now Iowa and wrote in their journals about the area's rich land. In 1682, French explorer René-Robert Cavelier, known as Sieur de La Salle, claimed a large area of central North America for France. He called the entire area Louisiana, after King Louis XIV of France. This area included present-day Iowa.

In 1788, a French Canadian miner named Julien Dubuque met the Mesquakie Indians in what is now Iowa. The Mesquakie allowed Dubuque to mine for lead there. This metal is used to make ammunition for guns. Dubuque lived in the Iowa area until his death in 1810. He is considered the first European settler in present-day Iowa.

The Louisiana Purchase

In 1803, France sold the Louisiana Territory to the United States. This sale is called the Louisiana Purchase. President Thomas Jefferson sent Meriwether Lewis and William Clark to explore the area. They traveled up the Missouri River in

1804, stopping in what is now Iowa. The group held a council with American Indians they met there.

The U.S. government decided to divide the Louisiana Purchase into smaller territories. At first, the land was divided into the Orleans Territory and the District of Louisiana. Iowa was part of the District of Louisiana. In 1812, the state of Louisiana was formed. Iowa became part of the renamed Missouri Territory. After Missouri became a state in 1821, Iowa did not have a government for several years.

Julien Dubuque was the first permanent European settler in Iowa.

Chief Black Hawk led the Sauk Indians in the early 1800s.

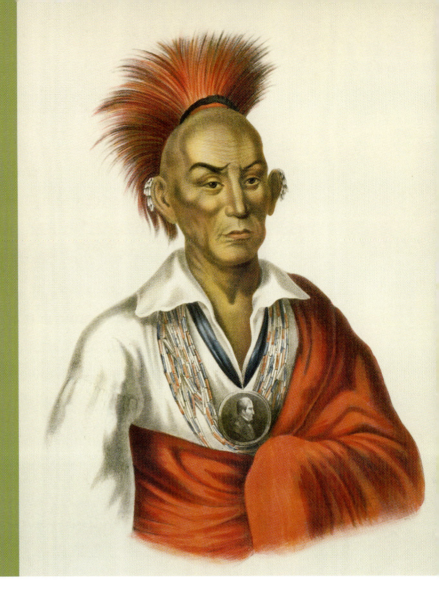

Black Hawk War

In 1829, the U.S. government forced some of the Sauk Indians west to a reservation in what is now Iowa. This action made room for white settlement in Illinois and in Wisconsin Territory. U.S. officials claimed the American Indians had sold them this land in an 1804 treaty.

"The white men do not scalp the head; but they do worse—they poison the heart . . . Farewell my nation! . . . Farewell to Black Hawk."
—Chief Black Hawk, in a surrender speech in 1832

Sauk Indian Chief Black Hawk disagreed with the U.S. government. Black Hawk had not signed the treaty. He told officials that the Indians who had signed the treaty did not speak for other Indian groups. Black Hawk's band was forced to move to Iowa in 1831.

Black Hawk and his followers returned to Illinois in 1832 to harvest corn. White settlers panicked at the sight of the American Indians. Illinois settlers asked the U.S. government to help drive away the Indians. The federal government sent soldiers to attack Black Hawk's group. Soldiers forced Black Hawk back to Iowa. Many Indians died in this conflict, which Europeans called the Black Hawk War. Chief Black Hawk surrendered and moved to the Iowa reservation.

Statehood and Settlement

In 1838, the U.S. government established Iowa Territory. This area of land included all of Iowa and chunks of present-day Minnesota and the Dakotas. At first, the territorial capital was Burlington. In 1841, Iowa City became the capital.

By 1844, the people of Iowa Territory wanted to become a state. In the beginning, Iowa delegates wanted the state to reach as far north as St. Paul, Minnesota. But Congress did not accept this plan. Finally, the delegates and Congress came to an agreement. The northern border of Iowa was set at its present-day location. On December 28, 1846, Iowa became the 29th state. Democrat Ansel Briggs became Iowa's first governor. At first, Iowa City was the state capital. In 1857, the more central location of Des Moines became the capital.

Railroads across Iowa increased transportation and helped the economy. This photo of the Des Moines Northern and Western Railroad was taken in 1887.

Safe Houses

In the mid-1800s, many African Americans escaping from slavery in the South traveled through Iowa. A system of safe houses called the "Underground Railroad" helped slaves escape safely to freedom.

Several famous safe houses were operated in Iowa. One stop was the home of James C. Jordan, shown here. Each day, Jordan hung a quilt outside his house to air. Escaping slaves knew it was safe to stop if the quilt had a black square sewn into it. Jordan's house still stands in West Des Moines.

After Iowa became a state, many pioneers hurried to settle the area. Pioneer families worked hard to build homes and prepare the soil for farming. They also built towns with schoolhouses, churches, and small businesses. Settlers battled natural hardships. They experienced windstorms, floods, and droughts. Prairie fires sometimes spread across the land, destroying houses and killing livestock.

Iowa's Railroads

By the late 1850s, a dozen railway lines ran into and out of Chicago. Iowa cities wanted to connect to the railways because railroads could deliver farm products faster than steamships could. Railroads could deliver produce before it spoiled.

Iowans hurried to set up a railway system throughout the state. In 1867, the first railroad crossed Iowa, from the Mississippi River to Council Bluffs.

Railroads helped Iowa's economy grow. Trains brought mail and other freight to small Iowa towns. The trains also carried shipments of corn, pork, and beef from small Iowa towns to Chicago and the East Coast. This link to large markets helped some Iowans establish successful businesses.

During the Great Depression, Iowa farm families did not have much to eat for Christmas dinner.

Prohibition

Many Iowans opposed drinking alcohol. In the 1800s and the early 1900s, laws were passed to stop the manufacture and sale of alcoholic drinks. Not all laws were enforced, and by 1915 all liquor laws in Iowa were withdrawn.

In 1920, the 18th Amendment to the U.S. Constitution stopped the sale of all alcoholic drinks in the United States. This practice was called Prohibition. Prohibition ended in 1933, and people could again legally buy alcohol. Iowa state law said alcohol sales were allowed, but voters in each county could decide whether to allow the sale of alcohol. It was not until 1963 that Iowans could drink alcoholic beverages in a restaurant or bar.

Economic Depression

Following World War I (1914–1918), the Iowa economy fell into depression in the 1920s. Land prices were high, so farmers went into debt to buy land. Prices for farm products went down, so farmers did not make much money. Banks had to take farms from farmers who could not pay back their loans. This process is called foreclosure. Some people lost their jobs and could not afford to pay their bills.

When the stock market crashed in 1929, the whole nation sank into the Great Depression (1929–1939). The drop in stock prices caused many banks to lose their money and close. Many people across the country lost their savings. Iowans continued to suffer low crop prices and to lose their jobs.

Some Iowa farmers joined the Farm Holiday Association (FHA). This group withheld products from the market to

Members of the Farm Holiday Association around the nation tipped over milk trucks. They hoped that if less milk were available, milk prices would increase.

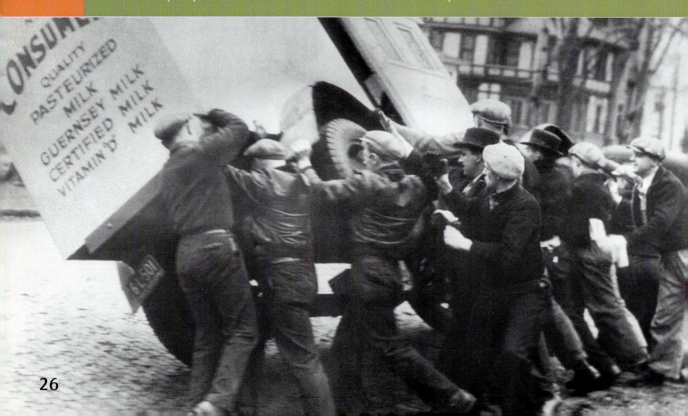

raise prices. This action angered people who could barely afford to buy milk and food at current prices. Violence sometimes occurred on FHA blockade lines. FHA members tipped over milk trucks and hijacked livestock trucks.

World War II

The United States entered World War II (1939–1945) in 1941 after the Japanese military attacked Pearl Harbor in Hawaii. About 286,000 Iowans served in the armed forces during the war. Other citizens worked at large ammunition plants in Ankeny and Burlington.

Many farm families grew food to send to troops. Iowa children planted Victory Gardens to raise as much food for their families as they could. Their gardens allowed more farm crops to be sent to troops overseas. The need for extra crops during the war ended the economic depression for farmers.

Late 1900s

After World War II, many countries wanted to improve ways to feed their people. Farmers needed hardy seeds that would stand up to heat and insects. Iowa native Norman Borlaug developed a type of wheat that resisted disease. This wheat increased food production. For his work, Borlaug was awarded the Nobel Peace Prize in 1970.

In the 1980s, Iowa's economy began to suffer. Crop prices dropped sharply, and Iowa's land values decreased. Small farmers were in danger of losing their farming businesses.

In the summer of 1993, Iowa experienced its worst natural disaster. It was called the Great Flood of 1993. Unusually high amounts of rain fell in the Midwest. The heavy rainfall caused rivers and streams to rise to dangerous levels. Iowa cities near rivers quickly became flooded. Water rose to street signs and forced people from their homes. The floodwaters

destroyed farmland and businesses. Iowa suffered millions of dollars in damages. Many Iowans needed years to recover from the flood.

By 1998, only about 100,000 family farms still existed in Iowa. This total was less than half the number of farms in the state just 50 years earlier. Farmers struggled to compete with large farming corporations. Many farmers were forced to take jobs outside the farm to support their families.

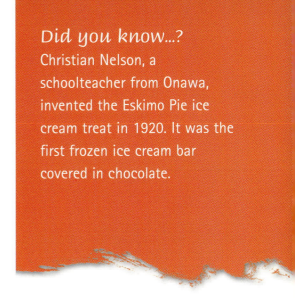

Did you know...?
Christian Nelson, a schoolteacher from Onawa, invented the Eskimo Pie ice cream treat in 1920. It was the first frozen ice cream bar covered in chocolate.

The Great Flood of 1993 left Des Moines and other cities covered in water.

Gold leaf covers the main dome on Iowa's capitol.

Chapter 4

Government and Politics

Iowa's present constitution was adopted in 1857. An earlier version of the constitution was written when Iowa became a state in 1846. Over the past 100 years, Iowa's constitution has been changed or added to about 40 times.

Branches of Government

Like most states, Iowa has three branches of government. These government sections are the executive, legislative, and judicial branches. Each branch provides checks and balances to the other branches. This system of government is patterned after the U.S. government.

"The politicians used to ask us [women] why we wanted the vote. They seemed to think that we want to do something particular with it, something we were not telling about. They did not understand that women wanted to help . . . the general welfare."
—Carrie Chapman Catt, suffragist

Iowa's governor is the leader of the executive branch. The governor is elected to a four-year term but can be reelected an unlimited number of times. The governor shares power with the legislative and judicial branches of Iowa's government. For example, a governor may sign or veto a bill the legislature has passed. In Iowa, the governor can approve most of a bill but veto parts of financial laws. This power is called the line-item veto.

The legislative branch, also called the General Assembly, is divided into two groups, a senate and a house of representatives. The senate has 50 members. The house of representatives has 100 members. Iowa's senate and house make the laws that govern the state. The legislature also decides how to spend Iowa's tax money.

Iowa's courts make up the judicial branch. The courts interpret laws. Iowa is divided into eight judicial districts. District judges are appointed by the governor. After serving one year, the district judges must be elected by the people.

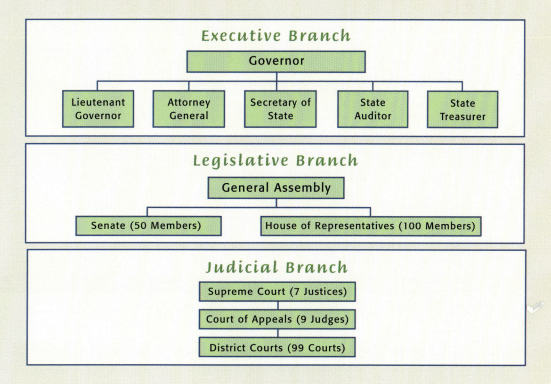

The Court of Appeals hears cases from the lower district courts. The Iowa Supreme Court is the highest court in the state.

Women's Rights

Iowan Carrie Chapman Catt led the fight for women's voting rights in the early 1900s. Until 1920, most states did not allow women to vote. Catt taught school in Iowa and became the first woman superintendent in Mason City. As the president of the National American Woman Suffrage Association, Catt spoke in support of women's rights. Her work helped the U.S. Congress pass the 19th Amendment in 1920, giving all women the right to vote. Catt also founded the League of Women Voters. This group educates voters about politics so they can make informed decisions when voting.

Carrie Chapman Catt was a famous suffragist from Iowa.

Herbert Hoover

Herbert Hoover was born on August 10, 1874, in West Branch, Iowa. Hoover's parents died when he was young, and he went to live with his uncle. He later became a mining engineer.

In 1929, Hoover became the 31st president of the United States. Hoover was president during the early years of the Great Depression. During this time, the nation's economy suffered. Many families struggled to survive. U.S. citizens looked to the federal government for help. Hoover believed that the economy would fix itself. But people lost faith in Hoover, and Franklin Delano Roosevelt won the presidency in the election of 1933.

Iowa Caucuses

Since 1972, Iowa has been the first state in the country to hold caucuses every year. Caucuses are small meetings held at the local level. The January before a presidential election, Democrats and Republicans each hold a caucus. Party members decide which candidates their parties will support for president and vice president.

> **Did you know…?**
> Governor James W. Grimes, who served from 1854 to 1858, is the only Iowa governor who was not a Democrat or Republican. Grimes was a member of the Whig Party.

Caucuses determine who will run in elections. The candidates from each party who win the most support at caucuses become the statewide nominees.

Because Iowa has the first caucuses, presidential and vice presidential candidates spend a great deal of time campaigning in the state. Candidates travel all over Iowa and hold meetings with Iowans in schools, churches, and even homes. The party members learn candidates' views on issues. Candidates who do well in Iowa caucuses often become the candidates of the national party.

Politics

Iowa's voter turnout usually is higher than the national average. As a state, Iowa has traditionally voted Republican. About three-fourths of the state's governors have been Republicans. About one-fourth have been Democrat. The state has voted for Democratic presidential candidates in the late 1900s.

Iowa congressional members have been involved in important national issues. Iowa democratic senator Tom Harkin played a major role in the 1999 impeachment trial of President

Republican George W. Bush campaigned in Cedar Rapids in 1999.

Bill Clinton. Harkin urged members of Congress to be objective in their decision of whether to impeach the president. Harkin believed congressional members should not just vote with their political party. Harkin has also played a national role in agricultural politics. In 2002, he helped pass a farm bill to benefit farmers in Iowa and other Midwestern states.

Iowa is the leading corn-producing state.

Chapter 5

Economy and Resources

Early business leaders in Iowa believed that Iowa's central location would be the key to its economic success. The state's industries link Iowa to the nation and the world. Iowa's economy is based on agriculture, manufacturing and mining, and service industries.

Agriculture

Iowa is a leading agricultural state. Farming brings about $12 billion each year to the state's economy. About 125,000 Iowans are farmers. This number is 8 percent of the state's workforce.

Iowa's 33.2 million acres (13.4 million hectares) of farmland support a large amount of crops. Iowa leads the country in corn production. The state grows 20 percent of the country's corn. Iowa farmers also produce 18 percent of the soybeans in the United States. Grains, peas, fruits, and vegetables also grow well in Iowa.

Livestock makes up the rest of Iowa's agriculture economy. Iowa is a leading producer of pork and beef. About 14 million

Hogs are Iowa's most common livestock. There are more than four times as many hogs as people in Iowa.

> **Did you know...?**
> In 1902, Iowans O. H. Benson and Jessie Field started two of the first 4-H clubs. They wanted kids to take pride in their farming heritage.

hogs live on Iowa farms. This number is 25 percent of all hogs produced in the United States. Iowa ranks among the top 10 states in raising beef and dairy cattle. Iowa farmers also raise sheep, turkey, and horses.

In recent years, some Iowa farmers have found other ways to earn money. They grow and sell flowers and Christmas trees. Growing other crops gives farmers another source of income in case some of their crops fail.

Manufacturing and Mining

Many of Iowa's manufacturing industries have close ties to agriculture. These companies produce a wide variety of food products, including popcorn, bacon, oatmeal, and packed meats. Quaker Oats in Cedar Rapids is one of the largest cereal mills in the world.

Iowa is the nation's leading pork processor. The state has 11 meatpacking plants that process about 2,500 hogs a day. Meatpacking plants provide 7 percent of Iowa's manufacturing jobs.

> **Did you know...?**
> Sac City in Iowa is considered the Popcorn Capital of the world. In 1995, the city created a popcorn ball 22 feet (7 meters) around that weighed 2,225 pounds (1,009 kilograms).

The smallest portion of Iowa's economy comes from mining. Only about 2,000 Iowa workers are miners. They mine limestone, sand, gravel, and clay.

Service Industries

Service industries earn about $30 billion for Iowa each year. This amount is 68 percent of the total value of goods and services produced in Iowa each year. Iowa's largest service industries are insurance, banking, and real estate.

Wholesale and retail businesses also are profitable service industries. Wholesalers sell large quantities of products to companies. Retail businesses include restaurants, grocery stores, and car dealerships. Many Iowa companies service and sell farm machinery.

Tourism also contributes to service industry income. During the summer months, tourists visit Iowa. They rent lakeside cabins, go hiking and camping, and visit the state fair. Some visit Living History Farms in Urbandale, where they can experience pioneer farming life.

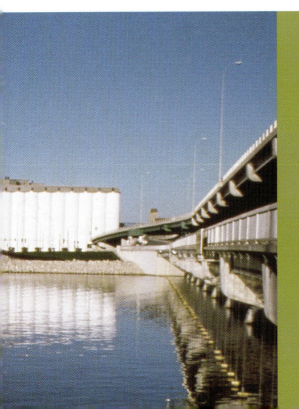

The Quaker Oats factory in Cedar Rapids is one of the largest cereal mills in the world.

Iowa's rural and city cultures come together at the Des Moines farmer's market.

Chapter 6

People and Culture

Although much of Iowa's land is used for farms, more than 90 percent of its people live in cities. The capital city of Des Moines is the state's largest city, with more than 450,000 people.

The People

In the late 1800s, many Iowans came from Germany, Ireland, Great Britain, and other countries. They immigrated to the United States and settled in Iowa. Today, most Iowans were born in the Hawkeye State.

Iowa's citizens have a variety of ethnic backgrounds. Most Iowans have German, Scandinavian, Irish, or British heritage.

"It is not the style of clothes one wears, neither the kind of automobile one drives, nor the amount of money one has in the bank, that counts. These mean nothing. It is simply service that measures success."
—George Washington Carver, scientist, Iowa State College's first African American faculty member

In the 1800s, these European families helped build Iowa's towns and cities. Today, 92.6 percent of Iowa's population is white. The other 7.4 percent is made up of African Americans, Hispanics, Asians, American Indians, and people of more than one race.

African Americans moved to Iowa after the Civil War (1861–1865). Most of them farmed. Some of their descendants live in southeastern Iowa. Later, some African Americans took jobs in Iowa's coal mines. By the 1920s, coal mining had decreased. African Americans then moved to larger cities to find jobs. Most worked in factories.

Des Moines, Davenport, Cedar Rapids, Waterloo, and other large cities are home to many of the state's minorities. Most Hispanic people came to Iowa from Mexico or Central America. Asian immigrants came from the Philippines, China, Japan, India, and Southeast Asia.

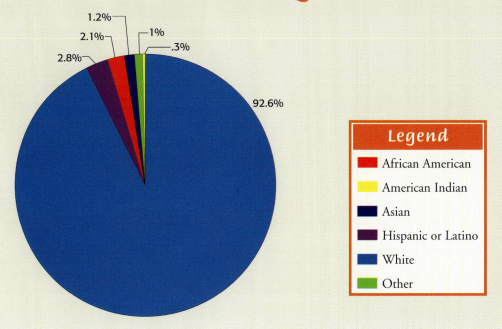

Most American Indians in Iowa are Mesquakie Indians. Many of these people live on 3,500 acres (1,416 hectares) of privately owned reservation land near Tama.

The Old Order Amish

The Old Order Amish families settled in several places throughout Iowa including Kalona, Hazleton, and Cresco. This religious group does not believe in a modern lifestyle

Grant Wood

Iowa's most famous artist is painter Grant Wood. In 1932, Wood established an art colony in Stone City. Wood's famous painting *American Gothic* features a farmer holding a pitchfork with a woman standing next to him. This woman is probably the man's daughter. The house that Wood used as the background of the painting still stands in Eldon.

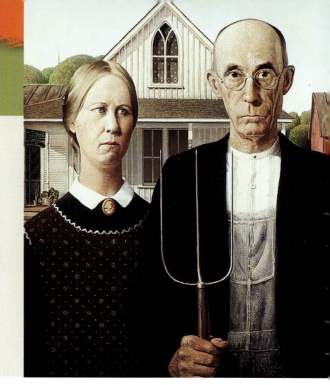

with electricity or cars. They drive horse-drawn buggies. They farm with horses and use plows along with other horse-drawn tools. The Amish have their own communities. They sometimes sell their homemade furniture and other items to people in nearby towns.

Iowa in Entertainment

Many famous actors and actresses were born in Iowa. Jerry Mathers played 7-year-old Theodore "Beaver" Cleaver on the popular 1950s TV series *Leave It to Beaver*. He was born in Sioux City in 1948. Donna Reed starred in *The Donna Reed*

> "I realized that all the really good ideas I'd ever had came to me while I was milking a cow. So I went back to Iowa."
>
> —Grant Wood, artist

Show, which aired from 1958 to 1966. She left her hometown of Denison for Los Angeles when she was just 16 years old. Reed also played Jimmy Stewart's wife, Mary, in the classic Christmas movie *It's a Wonderful Life*. Famous comedian and former *The Tonight Show* host Johnny Carson was born in Corning.

One of Iowa's best-known actors was John Wayne. Wayne starred as a cowboy in many classic western movies. Wayne's real name was Marion Morrison. He was born in the central Iowa town of Winterset.

Writers

Many famous writers have come from Iowa. Meredith Willson of Mason City wrote the popular Broadway musical *The Music Man*. The musical used Iowa as its setting. Ladora native Mildred Wirt Benson was the first of several authors to write the Nancy Drew mystery series. Benson became the first woman to earn a master's degree in journalism from the University of Iowa.

The Iowa Writers' Workshop at the University of Iowa is a well-respected school for writers. Created in 1936, it was the first university creative writing degree program. Other universities used the Iowa Writers' Workshop as a model for their own creative writing programs. Iowa Writers' Workshop graduates include best-selling novelist John Irving, Pulitzer Prize winner Jane Smiley, and short story writer Flannery O'Connor.

Iowa's Madison County was made famous in 1992, when author Robert James Waller published his romance novel *The*

Bridges of Madison County. Waller graduated with a doctorate from University of Iowa. He served as the dean of the University of Northern Iowa before publishing this book.

> **Did you know...?**
> Iowa has the highest literacy rate in the nation. More than 98 percent of Iowa's adult residents can read. Librarians and booksellers claim that Iowa residents read more books per person than any other state.

Food and Festivals

Iowa has a varied folklife. Iowans experience Mesquakie drumming, beadworking, and finger weaving, as well as Norwegian embroidery, fiddling, and

The covered bridges in Madison County, Iowa, became famous after Robert James Waller's novel *The Bridges of Madison County* was published.

> **Did you know…?**
> The 1989 movie *Field of Dreams* was filmed at a farm near Dyersville. A ballpark was made out of the farmer's cornfield.

foods. Iowans listen to African American blues and enjoy Danish folk dancing and old-time music.

Many of Iowa's towns hold festivals each year. The Tulip Festival in Pella celebrates the town's Dutch heritage. Nordic Fest, held in Decorah every July, celebrates the city's Scandinavian heritage.

The Iowa State Fair is one of the most famous state fairs in the United States. The first Iowa State Fair was held in 1854 in Fairfield, Iowa. Today, the Iowa State Fair is known throughout the world.

Held at the fairgrounds in Des Moines, the fair features traditional food and livestock competitions, farm machinery, and big entertainment shows in the grandstand. Visitors also view displays of award-winning food, photography, and art.

Iowa is a state that prides itself on its strong agricultural economy. It is known for its early caucuses in presidential election years. Iowa's citizens are proud to live in the heart of the Midwest.

Nearly 1 million people visit the 10-day Iowa State Fair. People enjoy competing in livestock competitions.

Recipe: Oven Caramel Corn

Iowa's corn is used for making corn syrup and other sweeteners. Popcorn is also grown in Iowa.

Ingredients

5 quarts (5 liters) popped popcorn
1 cup (240 mL) margarine
2 cups (480 mL) brown sugar
½ cup (120 mL) corn syrup
1 teaspoon (5 mL) salt
1 tablespoon (15 mL) vanilla flavoring
½ teaspoon (2.5 mL) baking soda

Equipment

roasting pan
measuring spoons
dry-ingredient measuring cups
medium saucepan
wooden spoon
oven mitts
airtight containers

What You Do

1. Preheat oven to 250°F (120°C).
2. Put the popped corn in roasting pan and set aside.
3. Combine margarine, brown sugar, corn syrup, and salt in a medium saucepan. Heat these ingredients over medium heat while stirring constantly. Let the mixture boil for 5 minutes.
4. Slowly add vanilla and baking soda to mixture in the saucepan. Stir.
5. Pour the mixture over the popcorn in the roasting pan and stir with a wooden spoon.
6. Place the roasting pan in the oven and bake caramel corn for 1 hour. Every 15 minutes, stir the popcorn again.
7. Store caramel corn in airtight containers.

Makes 20 1-cup (240-mL) servings

Iowa's Flag and Seal

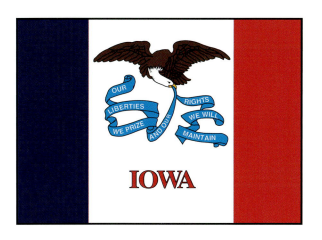

Iowa's Flag

Iowa's state legislature adopted the state flag in 1921. Iowa's state flag has three vertical bars. The blue bar represents loyalty, justice, and truth. The center white bar stands for purity, and the red bar stands for courage. In the center of the flag, an eagle holds a banner in its beak. The state motto is written on the banner.

Iowa's State Seal

Iowa's state seal was adopted in 1874. It features a soldier holding the American flag. The soldier stands in the middle of a wheat field, surrounded by farming and industrial equipment. In the background, a boat pushes its way along the Mississippi River. An eagle flies in the sky, carrying a streamer on which the state motto is printed.

Almanac

Eastern goldfinch

General Facts

Nickname: Hawkeye State

Population: 2,926,324 (U.S. Census 2000)

Population rank: 30th

Capital: Des Moines

Largest cities: Des Moines, Cedar Rapids, Davenport, Sioux City, Waterloo

Geography

Area: 56,276 square miles (145,755 square kilometers)

Size rank: 26th

Highest point: Hawkeye Point, 1,670 feet (509 meters) above sea level

Lowest point: Keokuk, 480 feet (146 meters) above sea level

Agriculture

Agricultural products: Corn, beef cattle, hogs, soybeans

Climate

Average summer temperature: 72 degrees Fahrenheit (22 degrees Celsius)

Average winter temperature: 21 degrees Fahrenheit (minus 6 degrees Celsius)

Average annual precipitation: 32 inches (81 centimeters)

Economy

Natural resources: Rich soil, limestone, sand, gravel

Types of industry: Meatpacking and food processing, rubber and plastic manufacturing, electronics, pharmaceuticals, machinery

Government

First governor: Ansel Briggs

Statehood: December 28, 1846; 29th state

U.S. Representatives: 5

U.S. Senators: 2

U.S. electoral votes: 7

Counties: 99

Symbols

Bird: Eastern goldfinch

Flower: Wild rose

Symbols

Motto: Our liberties we prize and our rights we will maintain.

Rock: Geode

Tree: Oak

Song: "Song of Iowa," by S. H. M. Byers

Wild rose

57

Timeline

State History

1600s
About 20 American Indian groups live in Iowa, including people of the Ioway, Sauk, and Mesquakie tribes.

1673
French explorers visit Iowa.

1788
Julien Dubuque becomes the first permanent European settler in Iowa.

1832
The Black Hawk War is fought.

1846
Iowa becomes a state on December 28.

1867
The first railroad across Iowa is completed in Council Bluffs.

U.S. History

1620
The Pilgrims establish a colony in North America.

1775–1783
American colonists fight for their independence from Great Britain in the Revolutionary War.

1812–1814
The United States and Great Britain fight the War of 1812.

1861–1865
The Civil War is fought between Northern and Southern states.

1920s
Land prices rise and crop prices fall, causing an economic depression among Iowa's farmers.

1936
The University of Iowa becomes the first university to offer a degree in creative writing; the Iowa Writers' Workshop is established.

1993
Many Iowa cities and large areas of farmland suffer damage from the Great Flood.

1980s
Iowa's economy suffers because of falling crop prices.

1929–1939
The U.S. economy suffers during the Great Depression.

1964
The U.S. Congress passes the Civil Rights Act, which makes discrimination illegal.

1939–1945
World War II is fought; the United States enters the war in 1941.

1914–1918
World War I is fought; the United States enters the war in 1917.

2001
On September 11, terrorists attack the World Trade Center and the Pentagon.

Words to Know

ammunition (am-yuh-NISH-uhn)—bullets and other objects that can be fired from weapons

bill (BIL)—a proposed plan for a new law

caucus (KAW-kuhss)—a local meeting of people who belong to a political party, usually to select candidates

erode (ee-RODE)—to gradually wear away; wind and water can erode soil.

folklife (FOHK-LIFE)—traditional culture, food, dance, music, and customs of a particular group of people

glacier (GLAY-shur)—a huge mass of slowly moving ice; glaciers often form in high mountain valleys where snow never completely melts.

line-item veto (LINE-EYE-tuhm VEE-toh)—a power held by the executive branch to pass part of a bill but deny certain financial parts of it

prehistoric (pree-hi-STOR-ik)—from a time before written history

suffragist (SUHF-ri-jist)—someone who believed in and worked for women's right to vote in the United States

To Learn More

Balcavage, Dynise. *Iowa.* From Sea to Shining Sea. New York: Children's Press, 2002.

Martin, Michael A. *Iowa: The Hawkeye State.* World Almanac Library of the States. Milwaukee: World Almanac Library, 2002.

Schwieder, Dorothy, Thomas Morain, and Lynn Nielsen. *Iowa Past to Present: The People and the Prairie.* Ames, Iowa: Iowa State Press, 2002.

Somervill, Barbara. *Votes for Women!: The Story of Carrie Chapman Catt.* Greensboro, N.C.: Morgan Reynolds, 2003.

Internet Sites

Track down many sites about Iowa.
Visit the FACT HOUND at *http://www.facthound.com*

IT IS EASY! IT IS FUN!
1) Go to *http://www.facthound.com*
2) Type in: 073681583X
3) Click on "FETCH IT" and FACT HOUND will find several links hand-picked by our editors.

Relax and let our pal FACT HOUND do the research for you!

Places to Write and Visit

Effigy Mounds National Monument
151 Highway 76
Harpers Ferry, IA 52146–7519

Iowa State Capitol
East Ninth and Grand Avenue
Des Moines, IA 50319

Living History Farms
2600 111th Street
Urbandale, IA 50322

Mississippi River Museum
Third Street Ice Harbor
P.O. Box 266
Dubuque, IA 52004–0266

National Balloon Museum
1601 North Jefferson
P.O. Box 149
Indianola, IA 50125

State Historical Society of Iowa
State of Iowa Historical Building
600 East Locust
Des Moines, IA 50319–0290

The *Des Moines Register's* Annual Great Bike Ride Across Iowa (RAGBRAI for short) is the nation's largest and oldest bike ride.

Index

actors, 48–49
agriculture, 9, 15, 27–28, 29, 38, 39–41, 52
Amish. See Old Order Amish

Black Hawk, Chief, 6, 20, 21
Black Hawk War, 6, 20–21
Borlaug, Norman, 27–28
Briggs, Ansel, 22

Catt, Carrie Chapman, 33–34
caucuses, 35–36
Central Lowlands, 9
climate, 13–14, 23, 28

Dissected Till Plains, 9, 10, 12
Driftless Area, 9, 10
Dubuque, Julien, 18, 19

economy, 22, 24, 25–27, 28, 35, 39–43
Effigy Mounds National Monument, 16
erosion, 15
explorers, 18
    Jolliet, Louis, 18
    La Salle, Rene-Robert Cavelier, Sieur de, 18
    Marquette, Jacques, 18

Farm Holiday Association, 26–27

farming. See agriculture
festivals, 51–52
flag, 55
food processing, 41, 43
Fox Indians. See Mesquakie (Fox) Indians

geode, 12
glaciers, 10
government (state), 19, 31–33
Great Depression, 26, 35
Great Flood of 1993, 28–29

Harkin, Tom, 36–37
Hoover, Herbert, 35

immigrants, 45–46
Iowa State Fair, 52, 53
Iowa Territory, 21–22
Ioway Indians, 17

Louisiana Purchase, 18–19

manufacturing and mining, 41–42
Mesquakie (Fox) Indians, 6, 17, 18, 47
Mound Builders, 17
movies, 49

National Balloon Classic, 4, 5
nickname, 6

Old Order Amish, 47–48

politics, 21–22, 33–34, 35–37
prairie, 8, 15
precipitation, 13, 28–29
Prohibition, 25

railroads, 22, 23–24

Sac and Fox, 6. See also Sauk Indians. See also Mesquakie (Fox) Indians
safe houses, 23
Sauk Indians, 6, 17, 20–21
seal, 55
service industries, 42–43
statehood, 21–22
storms, 14, 23

tourism, 12, 13, 43
TV shows, 48–49

weather. See climate, precipitation, storms
Wood, Grant, 48
World War II, 27
writers, 49–51

Young Drift Plains, 9, 10, 12